She Believed She Could, So She Did

*A Journal of Powerful Quotes from
Powerful Women*

ILLUSTRATED BY FLORA WAYCOTT

STERLING CHILDREN'S BOOKS
New York

STERLING CHILDREN'S BOOKS
New York

An Imprint of Sterling Publishing Co., Inc.
1166 Avenue of the Americas
New York, NY 10036

ISBN 978-1-4549-2837-9

Distributed in Canada by Sterling Publishing Co., Inc.
c/o Canadian Manda Group, 664 Annette Street
Toronto, Ontario, M6S 2C8, Canada
Distributed in the United Kingdom by GMC Distribution Services
Castle Place, 166 High Street, Lewes, East Sussex, BN7 1XU, England
Distributed in Australia by NewSouth Books
45 Beach Street, Coogee, NSW 2034, Australia

For information about custom editions, special sales, and premium and
corporate purchases, please contact Sterling Special Sales at 800-805-5489 or
specialsales@sterlingpublishing.com.

Manufactured in Canada

Lot #:
6 8 10 9 7 5
12/19

sterlingpublishing.com

Cover and interior design by Irene Vandervoort
Cover and interior illustrations by Flora Waycott

The artwork in this book was created using mixed media.

*T*he women who have made history include some of the most essential and influential people in our world. This journal is a celebration of these pioneers and the ideas that have helped them to persevere and succeed. Here is a space for you to write, reflect, and find inspiration in your own potential. Use their sage advice and motivational messages to plan for your future or ponder your present. Be nonjudgmental, be compassionate, and look to these quotes to clarify your thoughts as you go.

The women quoted on these pages are many things: tough, resilient, smart, ambitious, generous, and, above all, proud to be "she." We hope their quotes will inspire you to be proud of who you are, too.

"Do ordinary things with extraordinary love."

—MOTHER TERESA

Roman Catholic nun, missionary, and saint

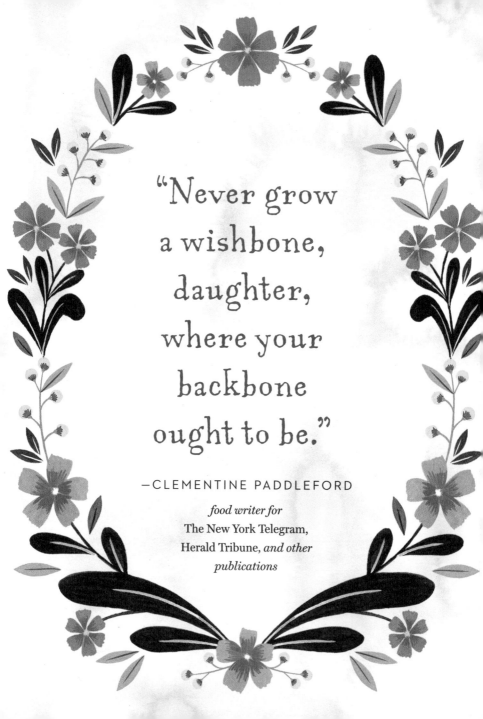

"Never grow
a wishbone,
daughter,
where your
backbone
ought to be."

—CLEMENTINE PADDLEFORD

food writer for
The New York Telegram,
Herald Tribune, *and other*
publications

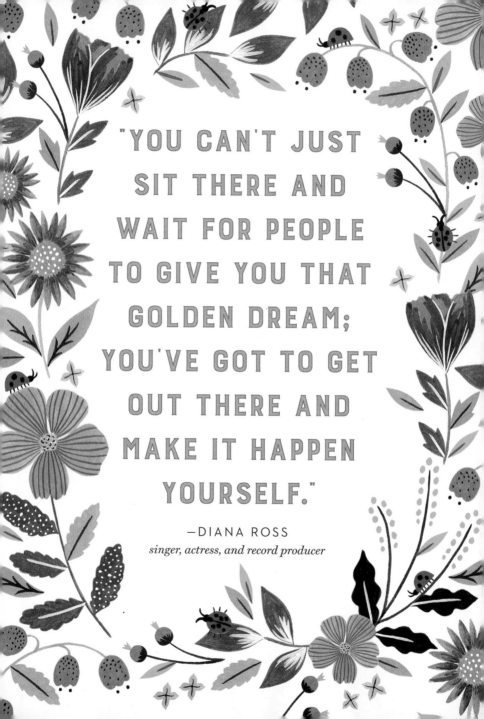

"YOU CAN'T JUST SIT THERE AND WAIT FOR PEOPLE TO GIVE YOU THAT GOLDEN DREAM; YOU'VE GOT TO GET OUT THERE AND MAKE IT HAPPEN YOURSELF."

—DIANA ROSS
singer, actress, and record producer

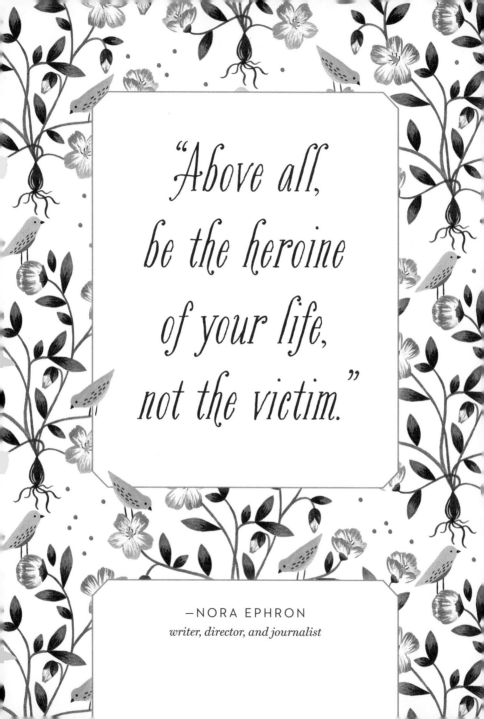

"Above all, be the heroine of your life, not the victim."

—NORA EPHRON
writer, director, and journalist

"Try to be
a rainbow in
someone's cloud."

—MAYA ANGELOU
poet and author

"You cannot shake hands with a clenched fist."

—INDIRA GANDHI
prime minister of India

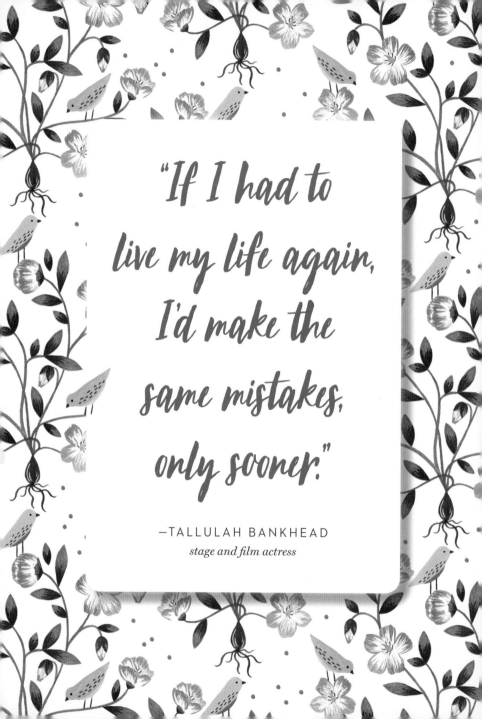

"If I had to live my life again, I'd make the same mistakes, only sooner."

—TALLULAH BANKHEAD
stage and film actress

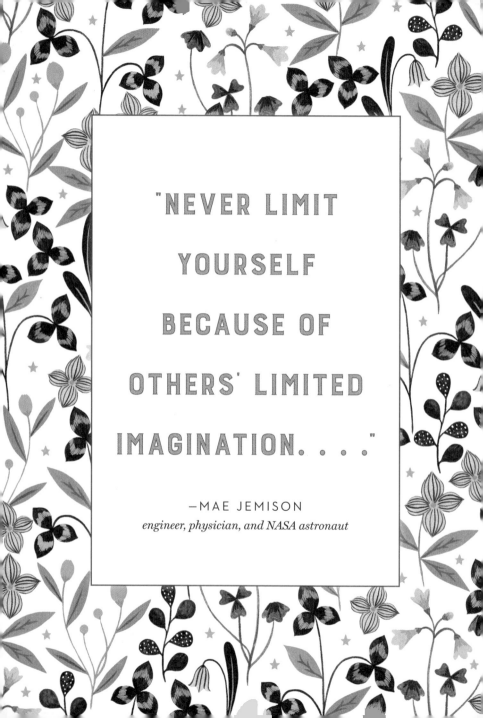

"NEVER LIMIT
YOURSELF
BECAUSE OF
OTHERS' LIMITED
IMAGINATION. . . ."

—MAE JEMISON
engineer, physician, and NASA astronaut

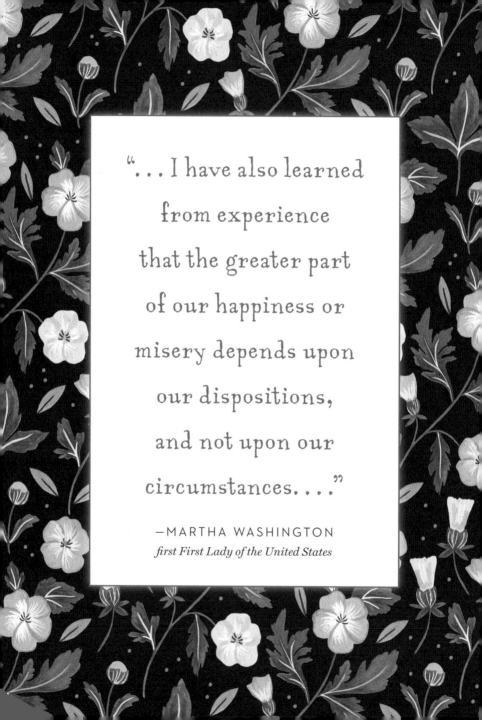

"... I have also learned from experience that the greater part of our happiness or misery depends upon our dispositions, and not upon our circumstances. ..."

—MARTHA WASHINGTON
first First Lady of the United States

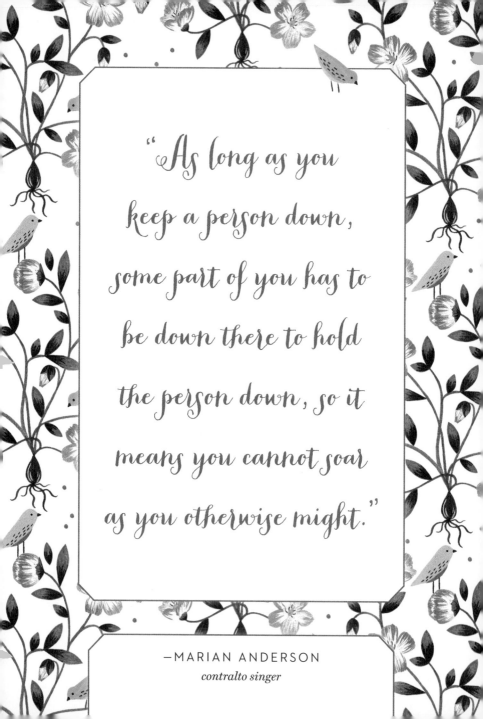

"As long as you keep a person down, some part of you has to be down there to hold the person down, so it means you cannot soar as you otherwise might."

—MARIAN ANDERSON

contralto singer

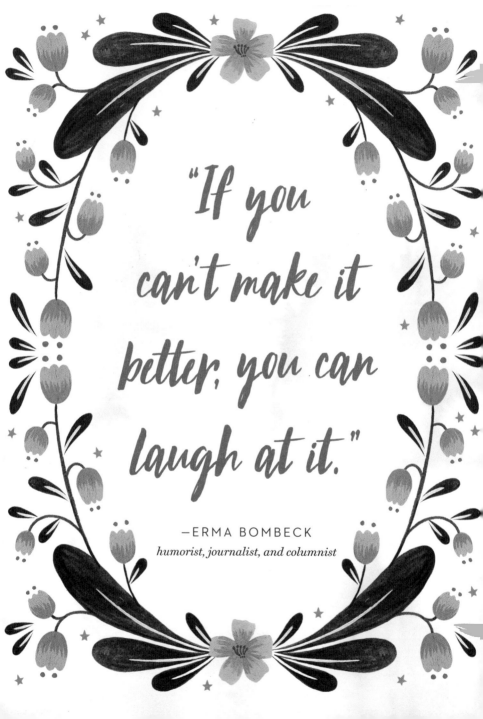

"If you can't make it better, you can laugh at it."

—ERMA BOMBECK
humorist, journalist, and columnist

"THE MOST
EFFECTIVE
WAY TO DO
IT IS
TO DO IT."

—AMELIA EARHART
aviator and pioneer

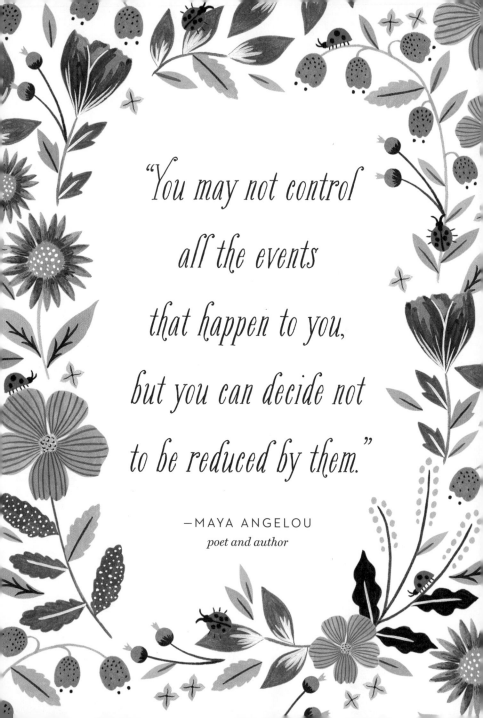

"You may not control all the events that happen to you, but you can decide not to be reduced by them."

—MAYA ANGELOU
poet and author

"How wonderful it is that nobody need wait a single moment before beginning to improve the world."

—ANNE FRANK
diarist and victim of the Holocaust

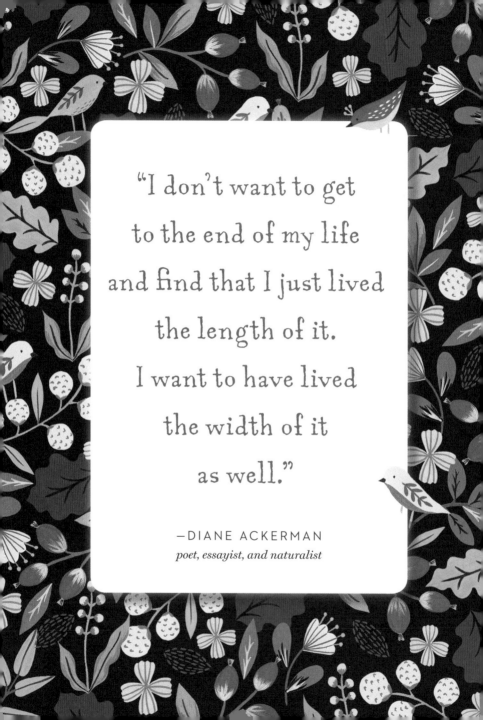

"I don't want to get
to the end of my life
and find that I just lived
the length of it.
I want to have lived
the width of it
as well."

—DIANE ACKERMAN

poet, essayist, and naturalist

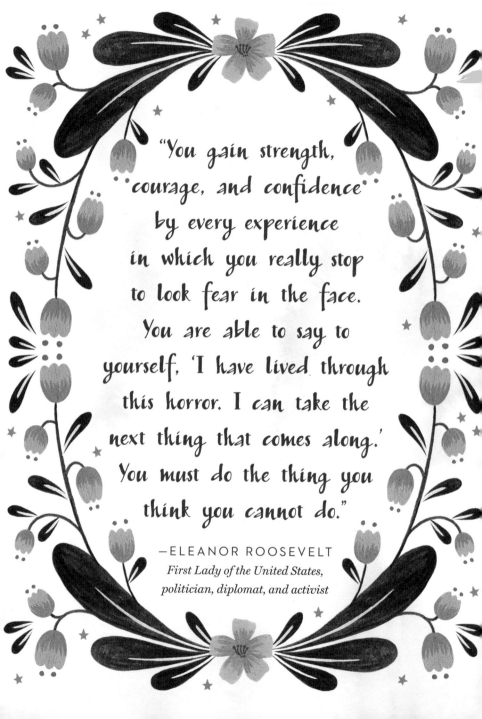

"You gain strength, courage, and confidence by every experience in which you really stop to look fear in the face. You are able to say to yourself, 'I have lived through this horror. I can take the next thing that comes along.' You must do the thing you think you cannot do."

—ELEANOR ROOSEVELT
First Lady of the United States, politician, diplomat, and activist

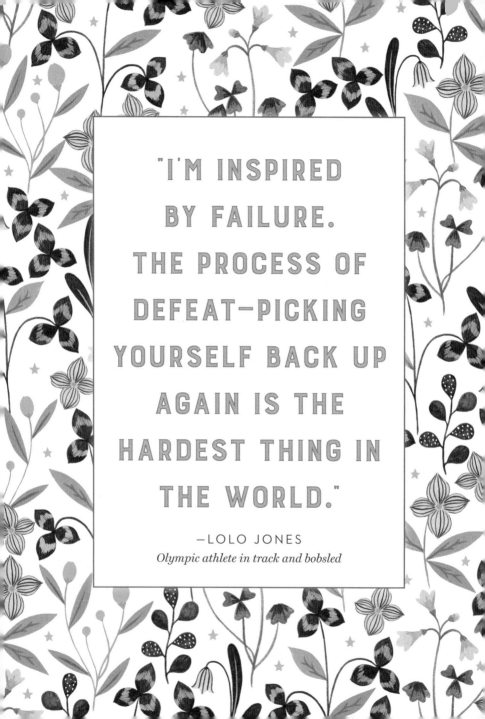

"I'M INSPIRED
BY FAILURE.
THE PROCESS OF
DEFEAT–PICKING
YOURSELF BACK UP
AGAIN IS THE
HARDEST THING IN
THE WORLD."

—LOLO JONES
Olympic athlete in track and bobsled

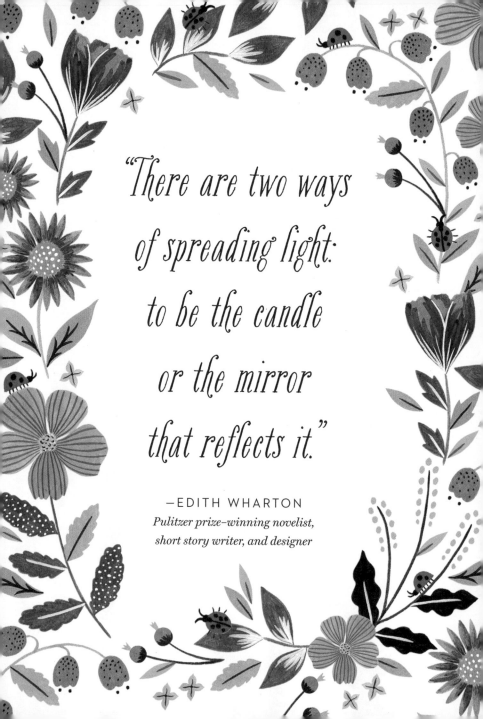

"There are two ways of spreading light: to be the candle or the mirror that reflects it."

—EDITH WHARTON
Pulitzer prize–winning novelist, short story writer, and designer

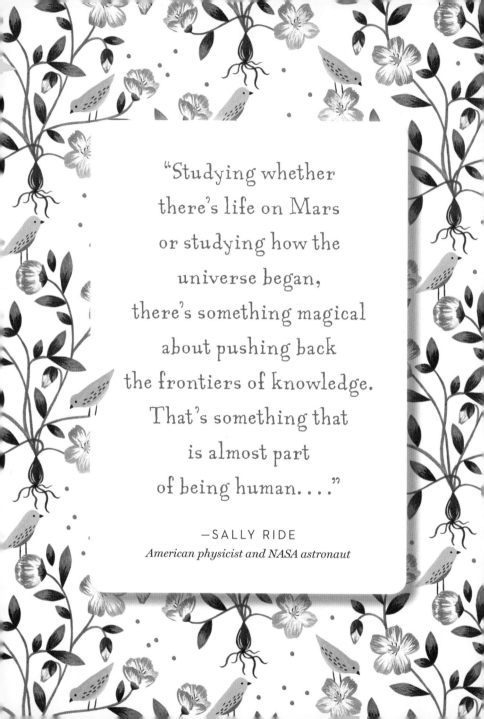

"Studying whether there's life on Mars or studying how the universe began, there's something magical about pushing back the frontiers of knowledge. That's something that is almost part of being human...."

—SALLY RIDE
American physicist and NASA astronaut

"The most courageous act is still to think for yourself. Aloud."

—COCO CHANEL
French fashion designer

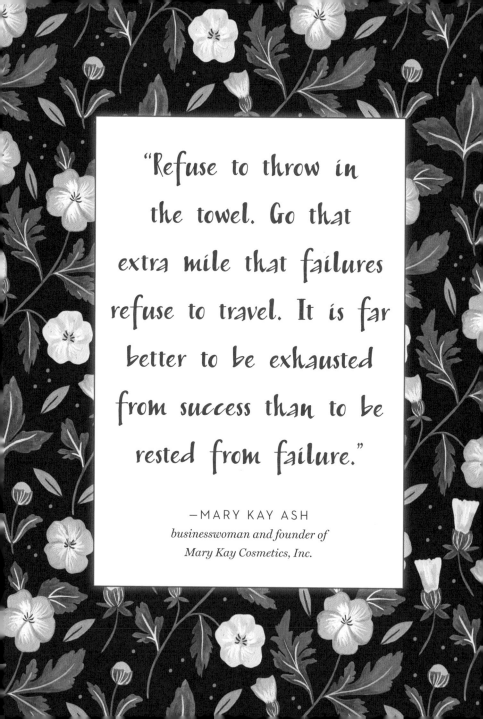

"Refuse to throw in the towel. Go that extra mile that failures refuse to travel. It is far better to be exhausted from success than to be rested from failure."

—MARY KAY ASH
businesswoman and founder of
Mary Kay Cosmetics, Inc.

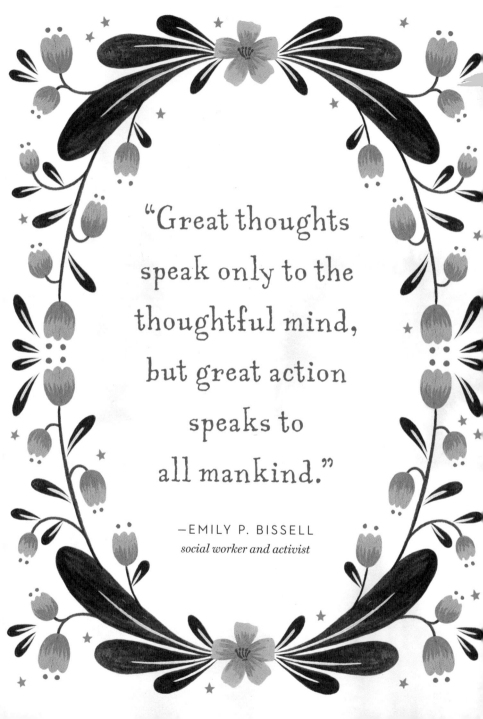

"Great thoughts speak only to the thoughtful mind, but great action speaks to all mankind."

—EMILY P. BISSELL
social worker and activist

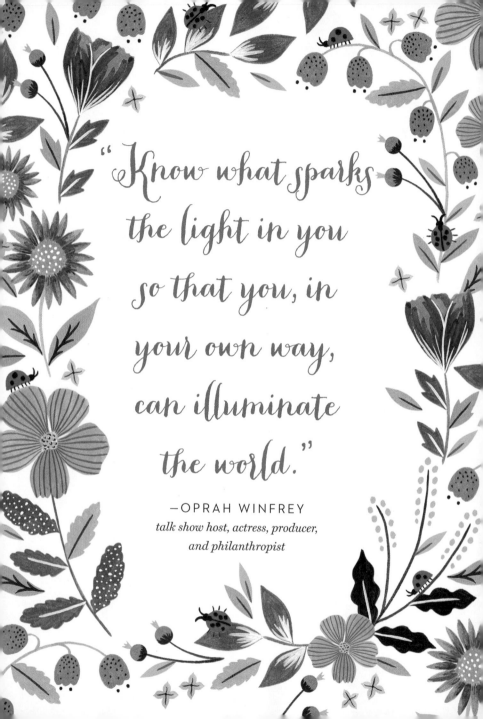

"Know what sparks the light in you so that you, in your own way, can illuminate the world."

—OPRAH WINFREY
talk show host, actress, producer, and philanthropist

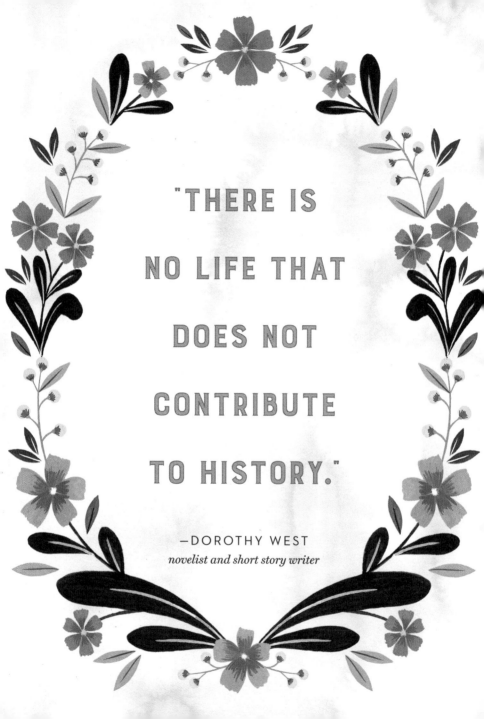

"THERE IS NO LIFE THAT DOES NOT CONTRIBUTE TO HISTORY."

—DOROTHY WEST
novelist and short story writer

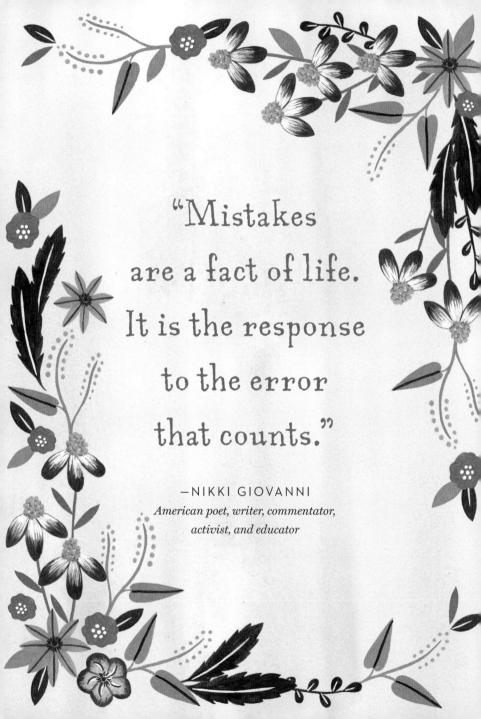

"Mistakes
are a fact of life.
It is the response
to the error
that counts."

—NIKKI GIOVANNI
*American poet, writer, commentator,
activist, and educator*

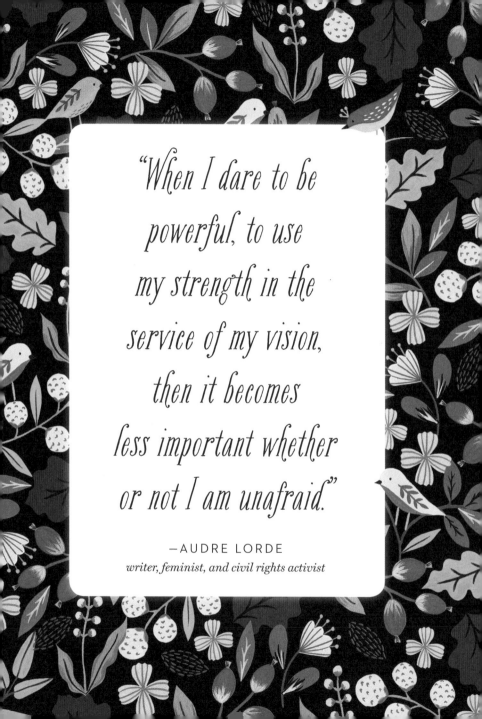

"When I dare to be powerful, to use my strength in the service of my vision, then it becomes less important whether or not I am unafraid."

—AUDRE LORDE
writer, feminist, and civil rights activist

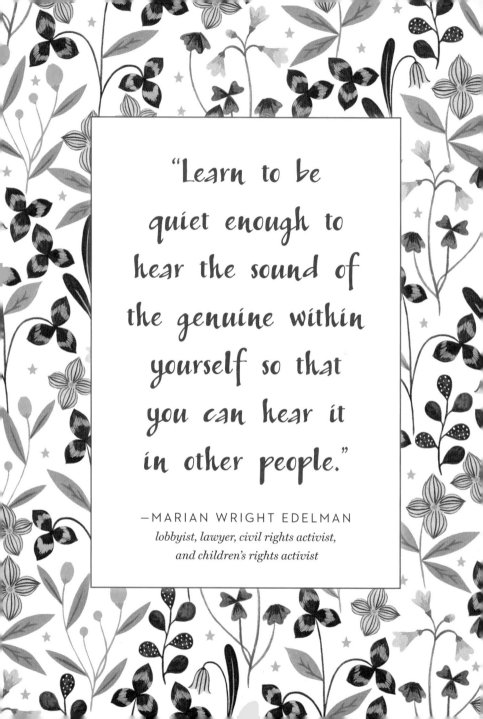

"Learn to be quiet enough to hear the sound of the genuine within yourself so that you can hear it in other people."

—MARIAN WRIGHT EDELMAN
lobbyist, lawyer, civil rights activist,
and children's rights activist

"The greatest gift is not being afraid to question."

—RUBY DEE

actress, poet, playwright, screenwriter,
journalist, and civil rights activist

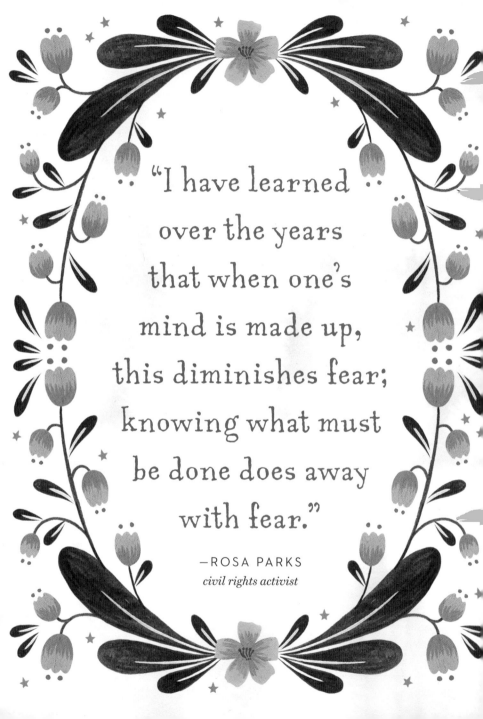

"I have learned over the years that when one's mind is made up, this diminishes fear; knowing what must be done does away with fear."

—ROSA PARKS
civil rights activist

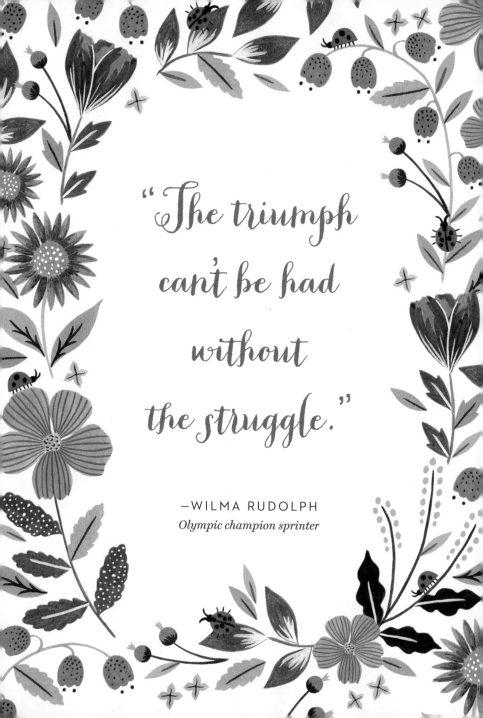

"The triumph can't be had without the struggle."

—WILMA RUDOLPH
Olympic champion sprinter

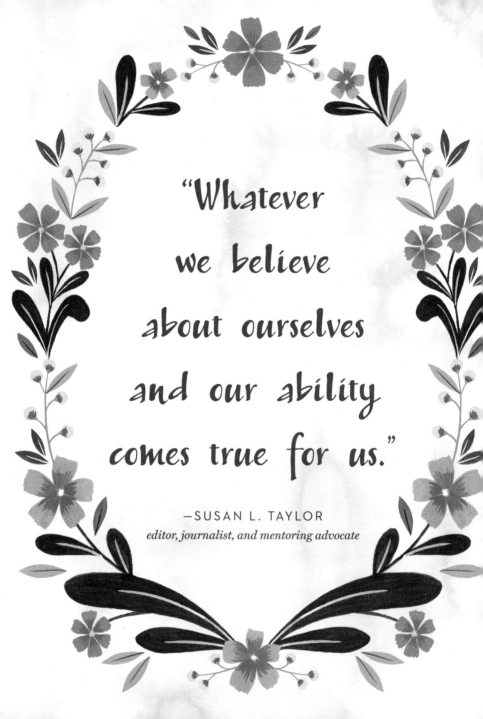

"Whatever we believe about ourselves and our ability comes true for us."

—SUSAN L. TAYLOR
editor, journalist, and mentoring advocate

"Always be a first-rate
version of yourself,
instead of a second-rate
version of somebody else."

—JUDY GARLAND
singer and actress

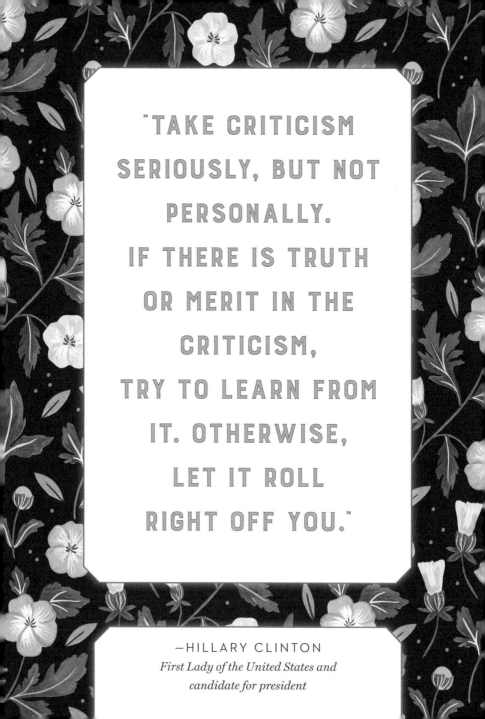

"TAKE CRITICISM SERIOUSLY, BUT NOT PERSONALLY. IF THERE IS TRUTH OR MERIT IN THE CRITICISM, TRY TO LEARN FROM IT. OTHERWISE, LET IT ROLL RIGHT OFF YOU."

—HILLARY CLINTON
*First Lady of the United States and
candidate for president*

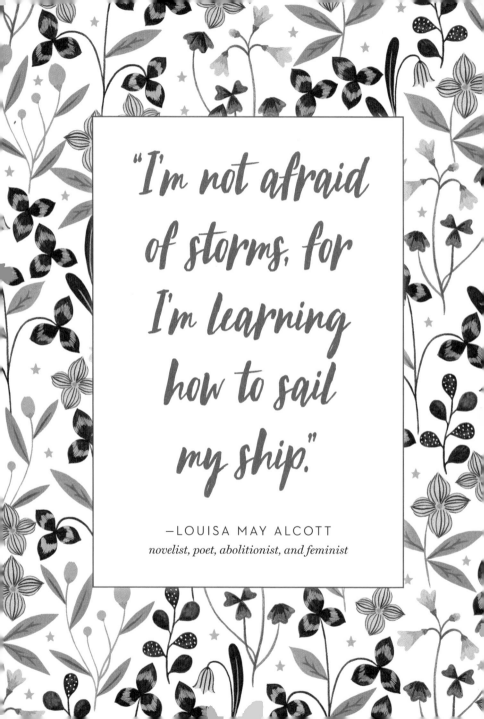

"I'm not afraid of storms, for I'm learning how to sail my ship."

—LOUISA MAY ALCOTT
novelist, poet, abolitionist, and feminist

....

....

....

....

....

....

....

....

....

....

....

....

....

....

....

....

....

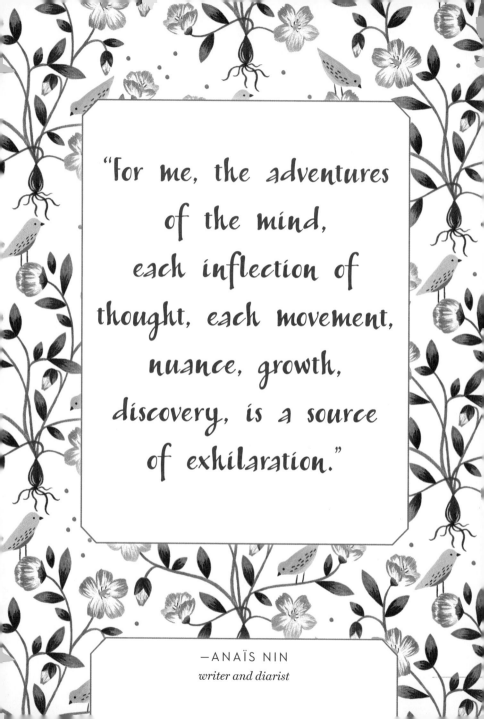

"For me, the adventures of the mind, each inflection of thought, each movement, nuance, growth, discovery, is a source of exhilaration."

—ANAÏS NIN
writer and diarist

"We do not need magic to transform our world. We carry all the power we need inside ourselves already. We have the power to imagine better."

—J. K. ROWLING
novelist, screenwriter, and film producer

"Without leaps of imagination, or dreaming, we lose the excitement of possibilities. Dreaming, after all, is a form of planning."

—GLORIA STEINEM
feminist, journalist, and social and political activist

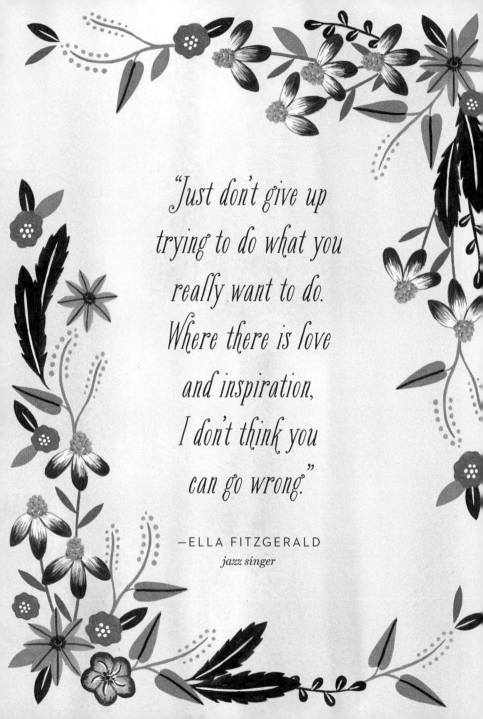

"Just don't give up
trying to do what you
really want to do.
Where there is love
and inspiration,
I don't think you
can go wrong."

—ELLA FITZGERALD
jazz singer

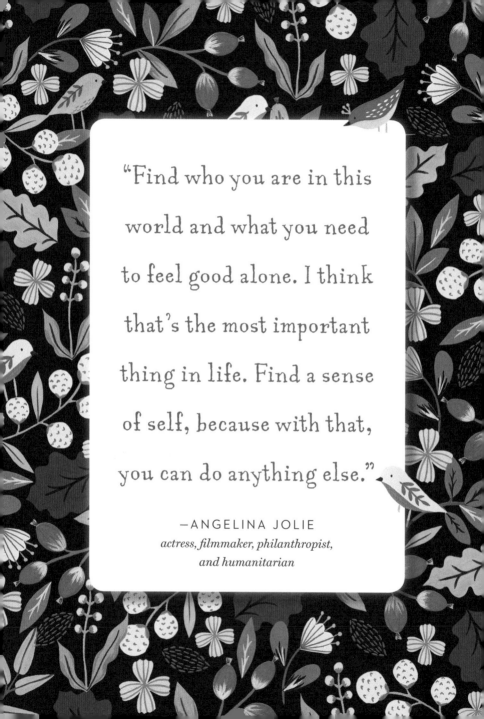

"Find who you are in this world and what you need to feel good alone. I think that's the most important thing in life. Find a sense of self, because with that, you can do anything else."

—ANGELINA JOLIE
actress, filmmaker, philanthropist, and humanitarian

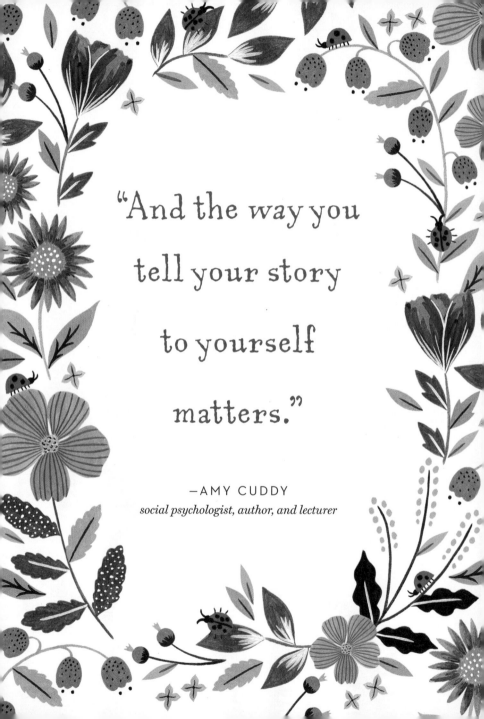

"And the way you tell your story to yourself matters."

—AMY CUDDY
social psychologist, author, and lecturer

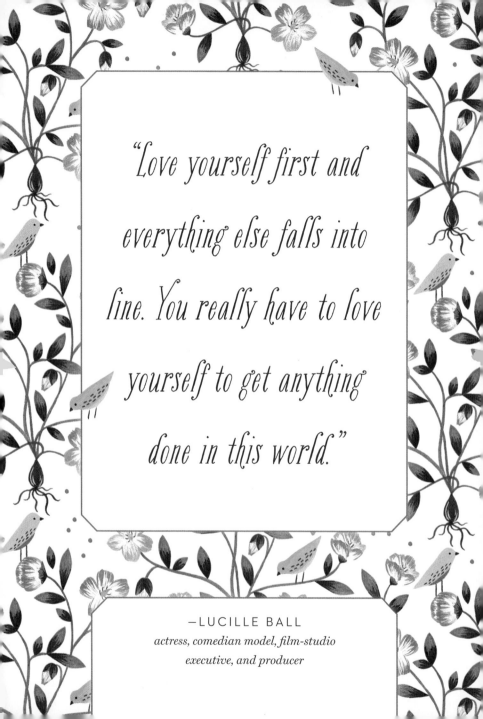

"Love yourself first and everything else falls into line. You really have to love yourself to get anything done in this world."

—LUCILLE BALL

actress, comedian model, film-studio
executive, and producer

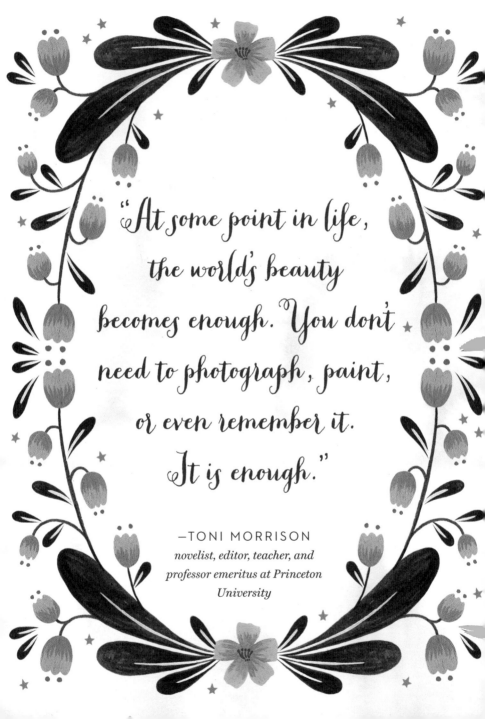

"At some point in life, the world's beauty becomes enough. You don't need to photograph, paint, or even remember it. It is enough."

—TONI MORRISON
novelist, editor, teacher, and professor emeritus at Princeton University

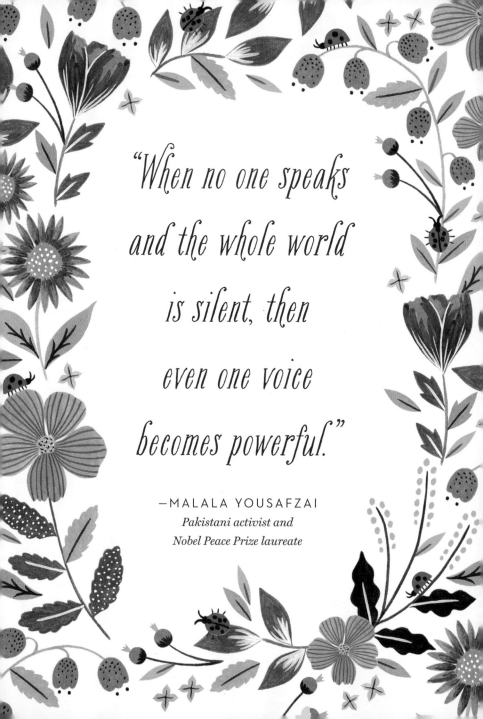

"When no one speaks
and the whole world
is silent, then
even one voice
becomes powerful."

—MALALA YOUSAFZAI
*Pakistani activist and
Nobel Peace Prize laureate*

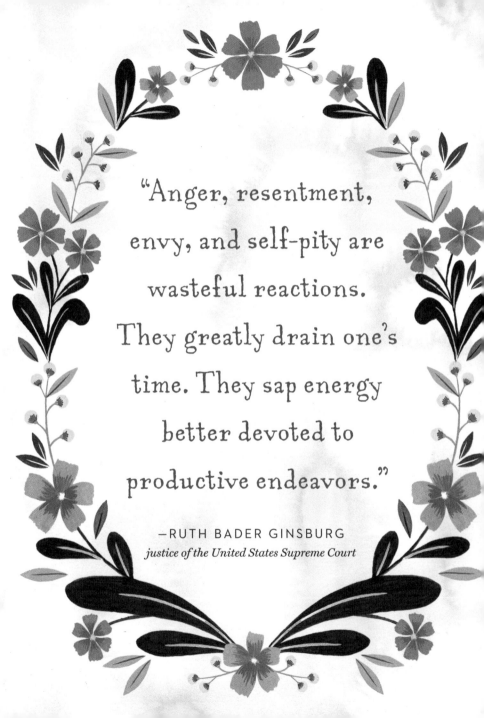

"Anger, resentment, envy, and self-pity are wasteful reactions. They greatly drain one's time. They sap energy better devoted to productive endeavors."

—RUTH BADER GINSBURG
justice of the United States Supreme Court

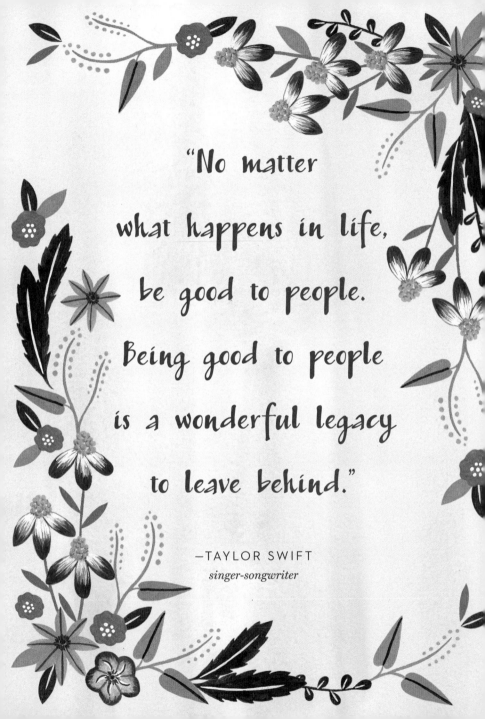

"No matter what happens in life, be good to people. Being good to people is a wonderful legacy to leave behind."

—TAYLOR SWIFT
singer-songwriter

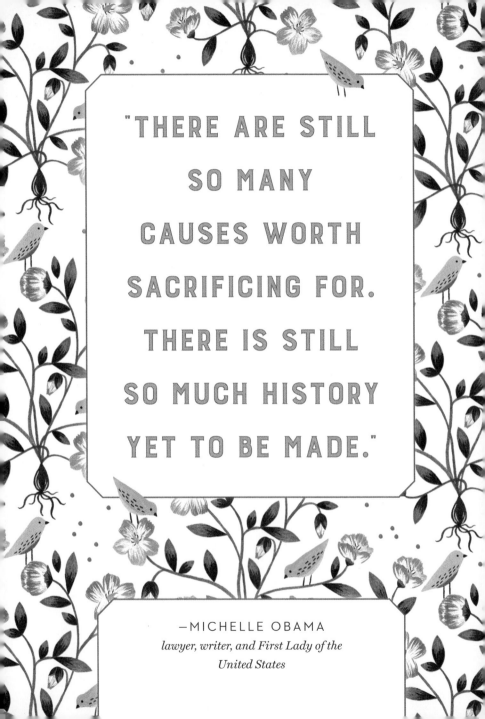

"THERE ARE STILL
SO MANY
CAUSES WORTH
SACRIFICING FOR.
THERE IS STILL
SO MUCH HISTORY
YET TO BE MADE."

—MICHELLE OBAMA
*lawyer, writer, and First Lady of the
United States*

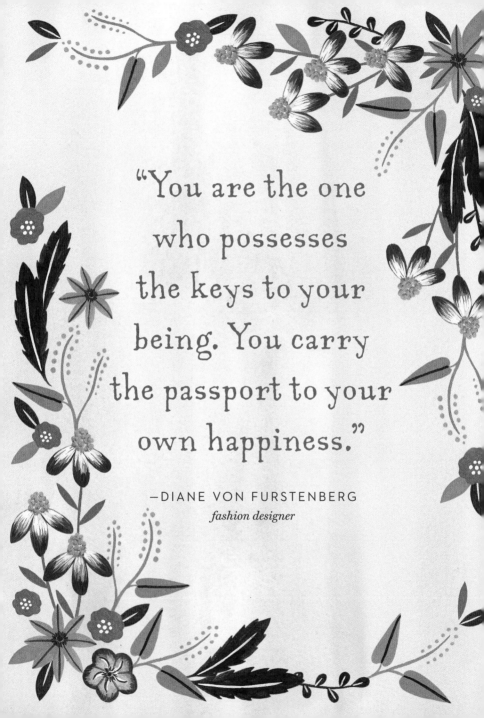

"You are the one who possesses the keys to your being. You carry the passport to your own happiness."

—DIANE VON FURSTENBERG
fashion designer

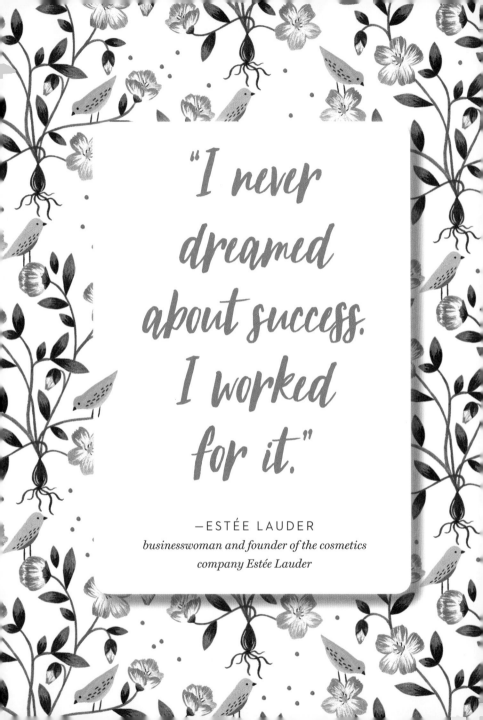

"I never dreamed about success. I worked for it."

—ESTÉE LAUDER
businesswoman and founder of the cosmetics company Estée Lauder

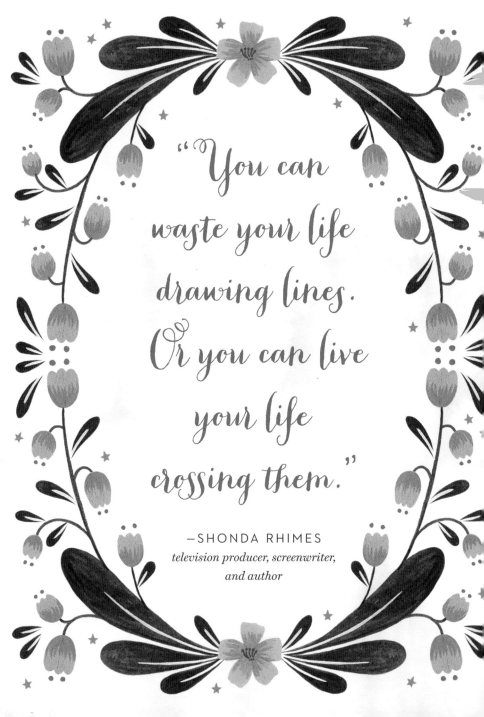

"You can waste your life drawing lines. Or you can live your life crossing them."

—SHONDA RHIMES
*television producer, screenwriter,
and author*

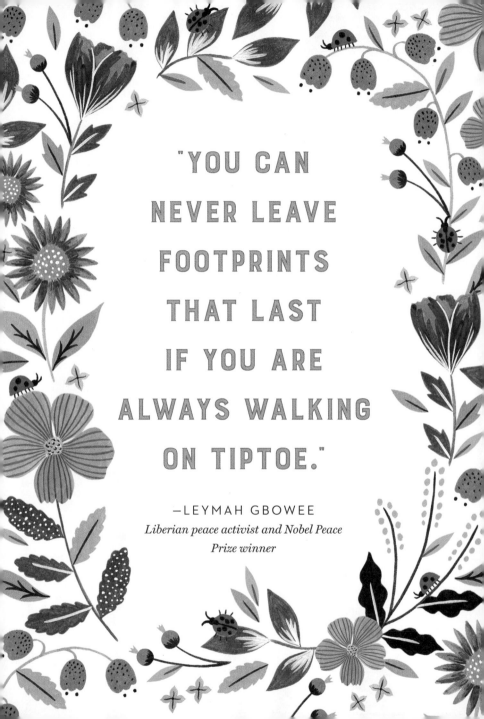

"YOU CAN NEVER LEAVE FOOTPRINTS THAT LAST IF YOU ARE ALWAYS WALKING ON TIPTOE."

—LEYMAH GBOWEE
Liberian peace activist and Nobel Peace Prize winner

"If you don't like the road you're walking, start paving another one."

—DOLLY PARTON
singer, songwriter, musician, record producer, actress, author, businesswoman, and philanthropist

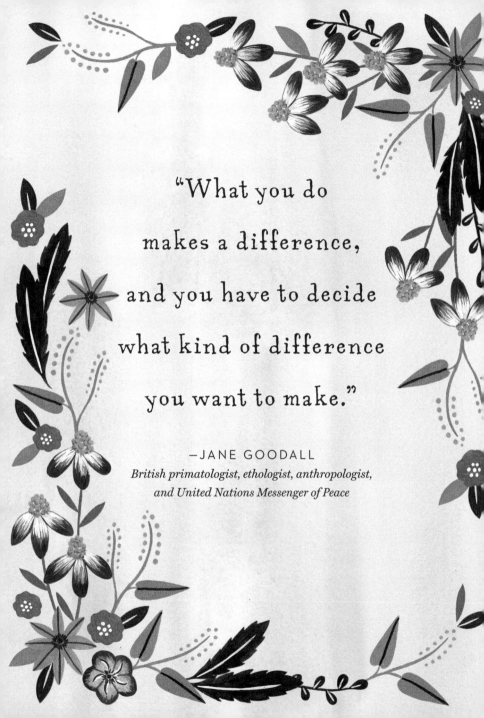

"What you do makes a difference, and you have to decide what kind of difference you want to make."

—JANE GOODALL
*British primatologist, ethologist, anthropologist,
and United Nations Messenger of Peace*

"Be open to learning new lessons even if they contradict the lessons you learned yesterday."

—ELLEN DEGENERES
comedian, television host, actress, writer, and producer

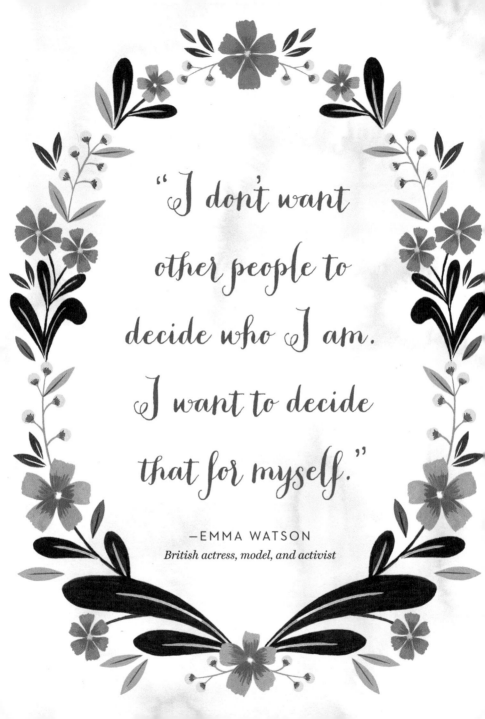

"I don't want other people to decide who I am. I want to decide that for myself."

—EMMA WATSON
British actress, model, and activist

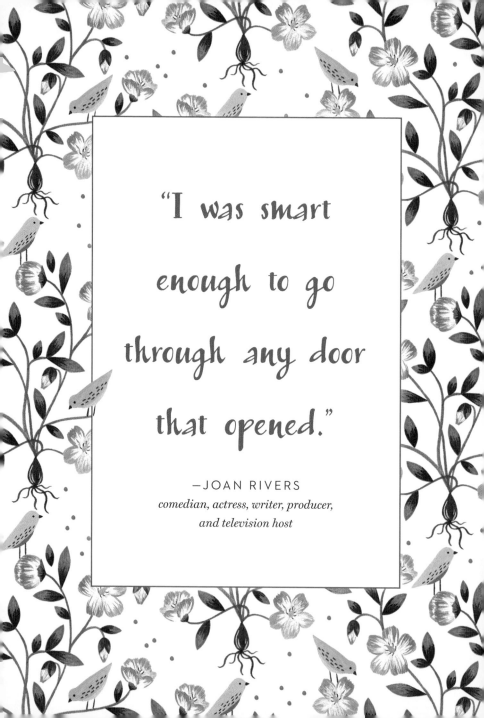

"I was smart enough to go through any door that opened."

—JOAN RIVERS
comedian, actress, writer, producer, and television host

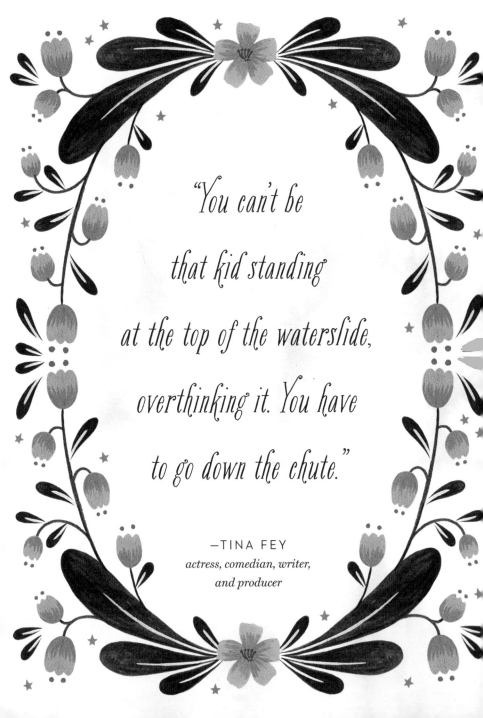

"You can't be
that kid standing
at the top of the waterslide,
overthinking it. You have
to go down the chute."

—TINA FEY
*actress, comedian, writer,
and producer*

"Make the most of yourself by fanning the tiny, inner sparks of possibility into flames of achievement."

—GOLDA MEIR
Israeli teacher, stateswoman, politician, and prime minister of Israel

"DON'T LOOK
AT YOUR FEET
TO SEE IF YOU ARE
DOING IT RIGHT.
JUST DANCE."

—ANNE LAMOTT
*novelist, non-fiction writer, political activist,
and public speaker*

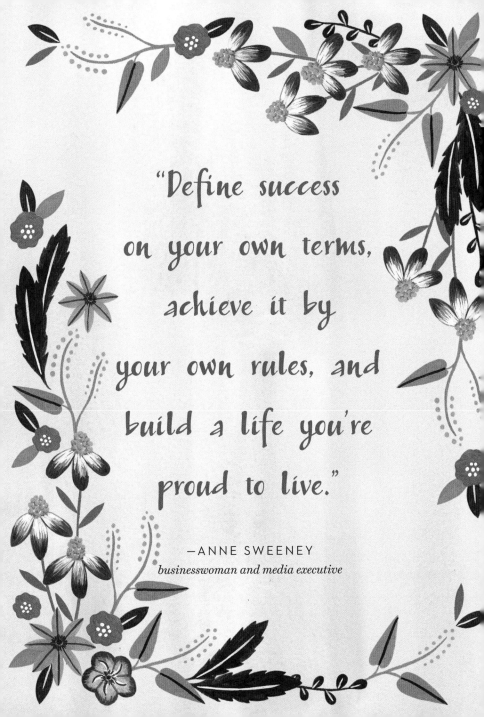

"Define success on your own terms, achieve it by your own rules, and build a life you're proud to live."

—ANNE SWEENEY
businesswoman and media executive

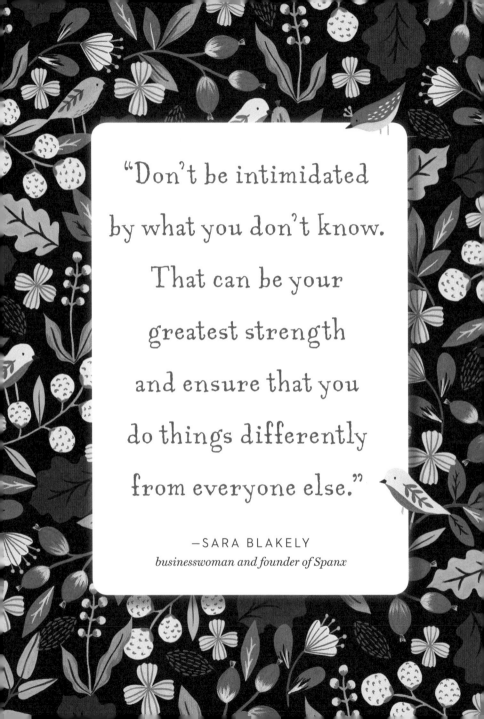

"Don't be intimidated by what you don't know. That can be your greatest strength and ensure that you do things differently from everyone else."

—SARA BLAKELY
businesswoman and founder of Spanx

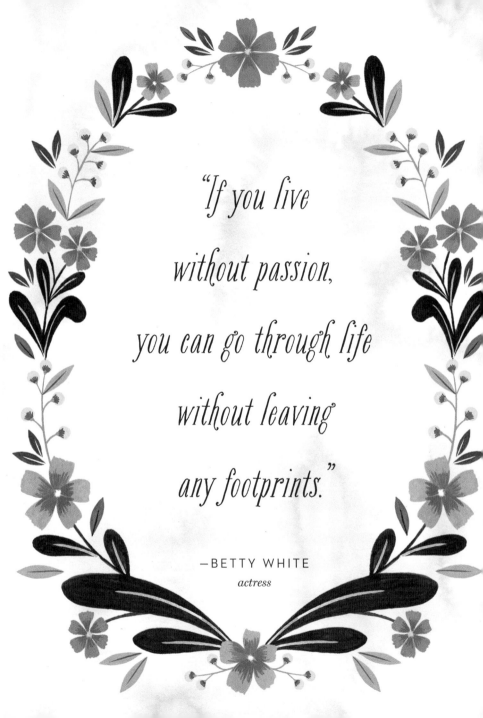

"If you live without passion, you can go through life without leaving any footprints."

—BETTY WHITE
actress

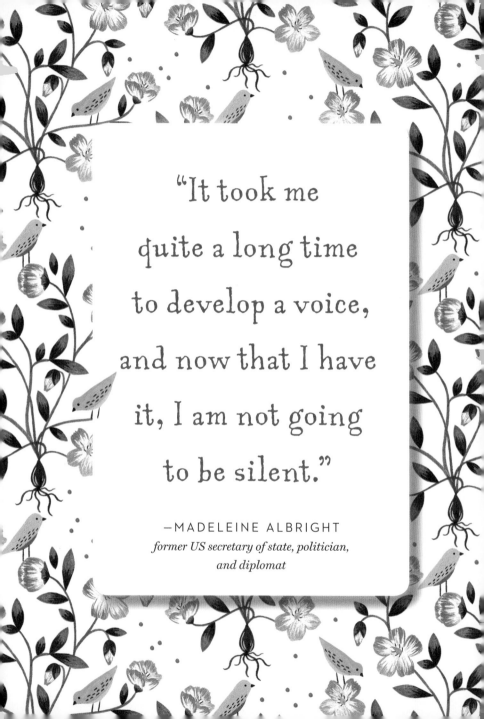

"It took me
quite a long time
to develop a voice,
and now that I have
it, I am not going
to be silent."

—MADELEINE ALBRIGHT
*former US secretary of state, politician,
and diplomat*

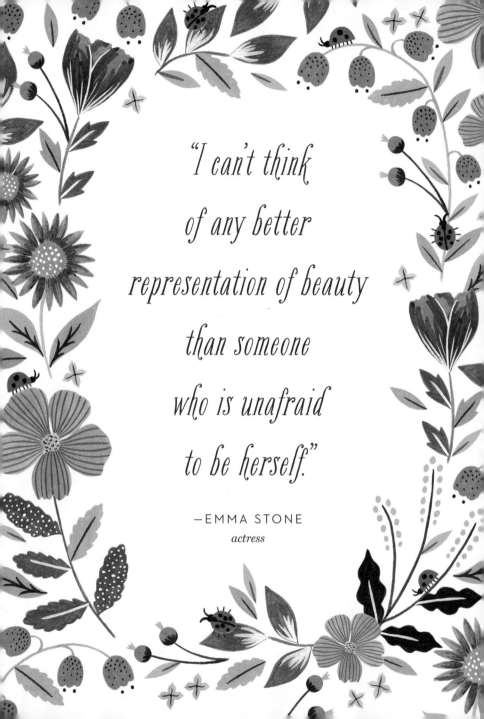

"I can't think of any better representation of beauty than someone who is unafraid to be herself."

—EMMA STONE

actress

"You really have to have a goal. The goalposts might shift, but you should have a goal."

—ZAHA HADID
Iraqi-British architect

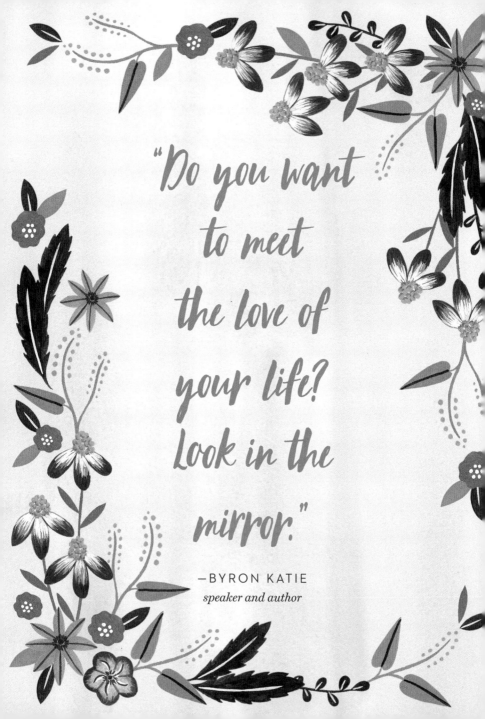

"Do you want to meet the love of your life? Look in the mirror."

—BYRON KATIE
speaker and author

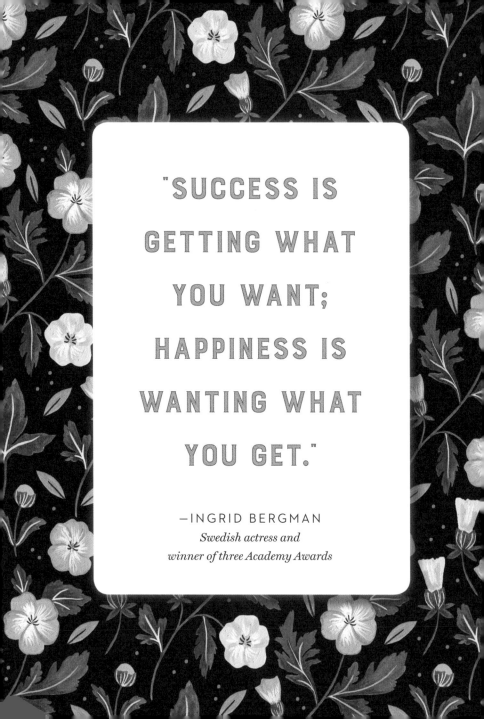

"SUCCESS IS GETTING WHAT YOU WANT; HAPPINESS IS WANTING WHAT YOU GET."

—INGRID BERGMAN
*Swedish actress and
winner of three Academy Awards*

"...if you don't risk anything, you risk even more."

—ERICA JONG
novelist and poet

"Not knowing you can't do something is sometimes all it takes to do it."

—ALLY CARTER
author of young adult fiction and adult fiction

"One's life has value
so long as one attributes
value to the life of others,
by means of love, friendship,
indignation, and compassion."

—SIMONE DE BEAUVOIR
*French writer, existentialist philosopher,
political activist, and feminist*

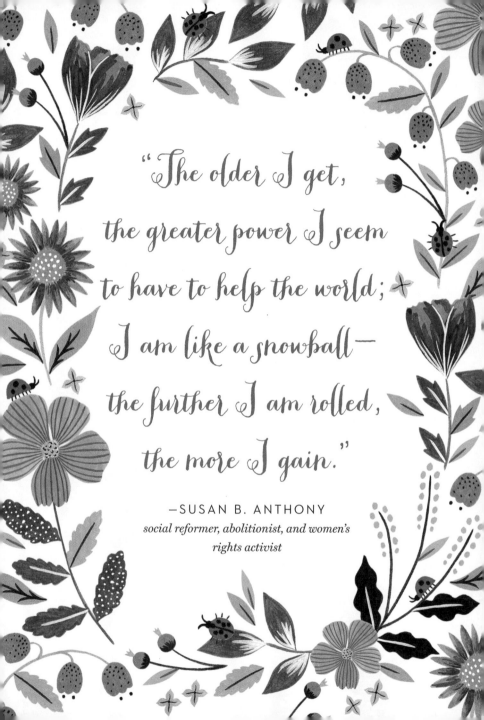

"The older I get,
the greater power I seem
to have to help the world;
I am like a snowball—
the further I am rolled,
the more I gain."

—SUSAN B. ANTHONY
*social reformer, abolitionist, and women's
rights activist*

"It is not easy

to be a pioneer—but

oh, it is fascinating!"

—ELIZABETH BLACKWELL

*British-born physician, first woman to receive
a medical degree in the United States, as well as
the first woman on the UK Medical Register*

"SAYING

NOTHING . . .

SOMETIMES

SAYS THE MOST."

—EMILY DICKINSON

poet

....

....

....

....

....

....

....

....

....

....

....

....

....

....

....

"You must want!
You have the
right to ask!
You must desire."

—EVA PERÓN
First Lady of Argentina

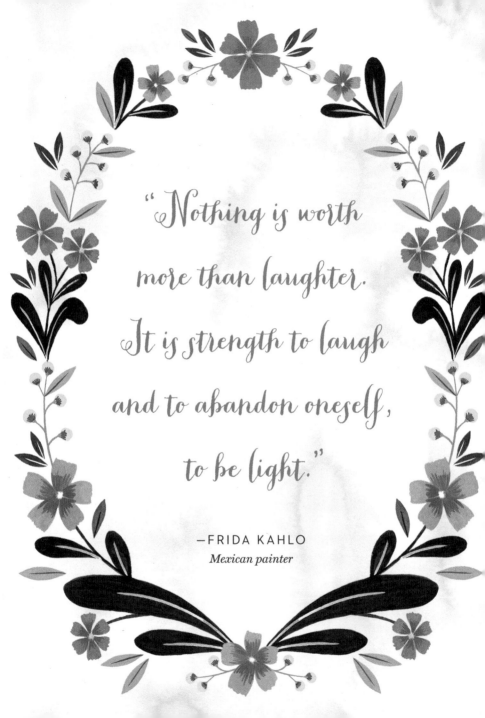

"Nothing is worth
more than laughter.
It is strength to laugh
and to abandon oneself,
to be light."

—FRIDA KAHLO
Mexican painter

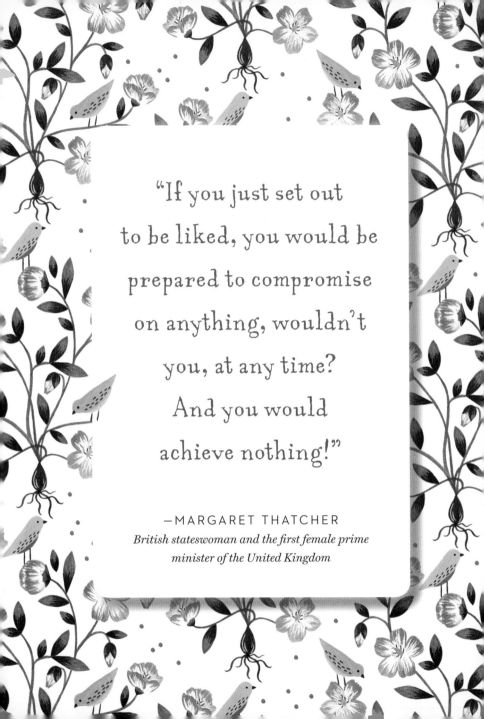

"If you just set out
to be liked, you would be
prepared to compromise
on anything, wouldn't
you, at any time?
And you would
achieve nothing!"

—MARGARET THATCHER
*British stateswoman and the first female prime
minister of the United Kingdom*

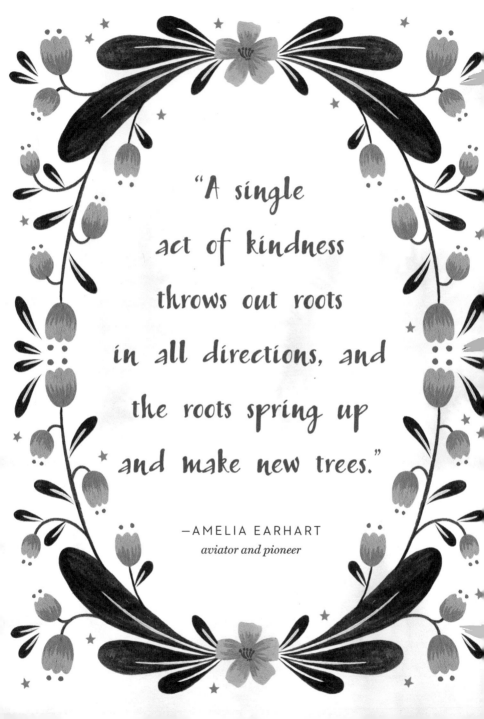

"A single
act of kindness
throws out roots
in all directions, and
the roots spring up
and make new trees."

—AMELIA EARHART
aviator and pioneer

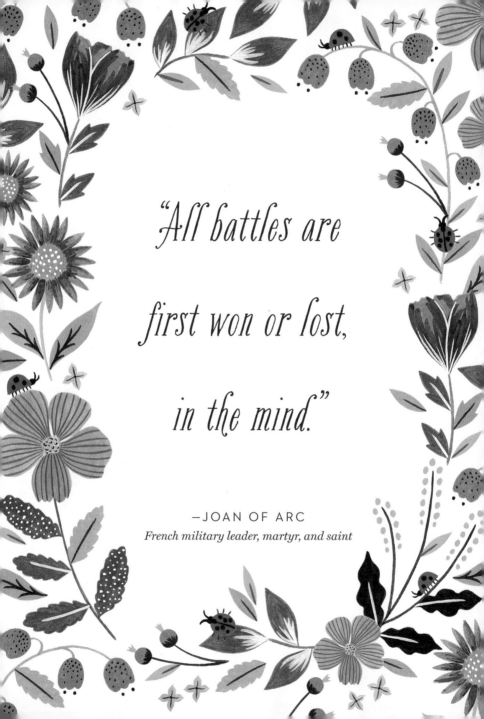

"All battles are first won or lost, in the mind."

—JOAN OF ARC
French military leader, martyr, and saint

"We must believe that we are gifted for something, and that this thing, at whatever cost, must be attained."

—MARIE CURIE
Polish and naturalized French physicist and chemist

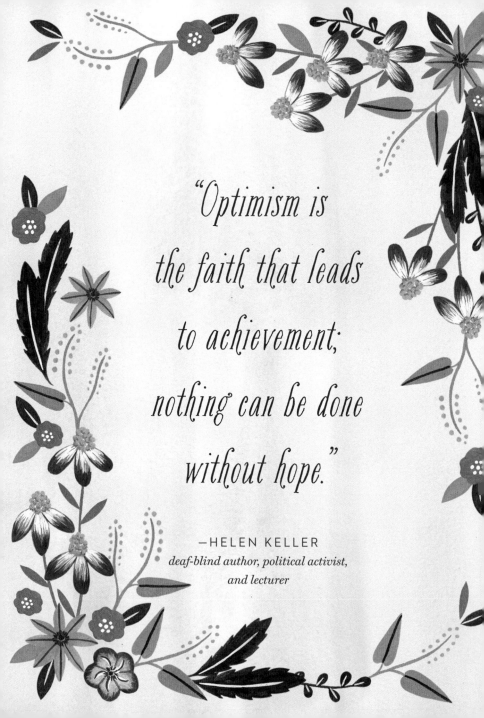

"Optimism is
the faith that leads
to achievement;
nothing can be done
without hope."

—HELEN KELLER
*deaf-blind author, political activist,
and lecturer*

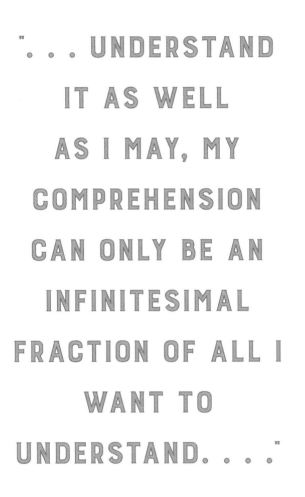

"...UNDERSTAND IT AS WELL AS I MAY, MY COMPREHENSION CAN ONLY BE AN INFINITESIMAL FRACTION OF ALL I WANT TO UNDERSTAND...."

—ADA LOVELACE

English mathematician and writer

"There is only
one of you in the world,
just one, and if that is
not fulfilled, then something
has been lost."

—MARTHA GRAHAM
modern dancer and choreographer

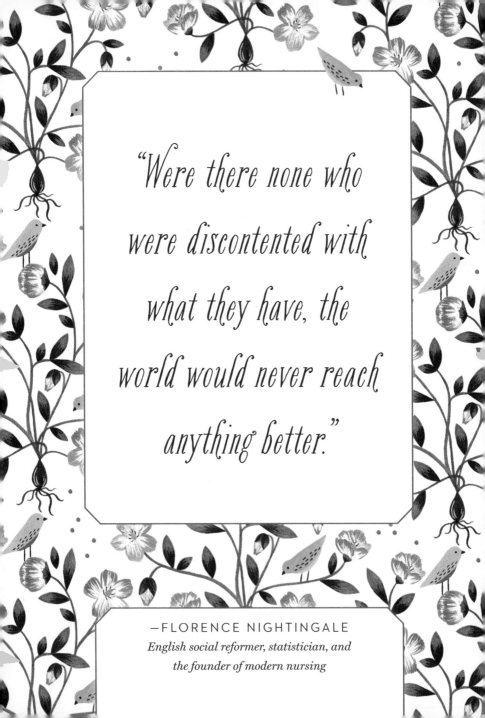

"Were there none who were discontented with what they have, the world would never reach anything better."

—FLORENCE NIGHTINGALE

English social reformer, statistician, and the founder of modern nursing

"Find something you're passionate about and keep tremendously interested in it."

—JULIA CHILD
chef, author, and television personality

"Many awful things have been done in the name of love, but nothing awful can be done in the name of respect."

—MAGDA GERBER
Hungarian-born early childhood educator

"The path to your success is not as fixed and inflexible as you think."

—MISTY COPELAND
ballet dancer, author, and motivational speaker

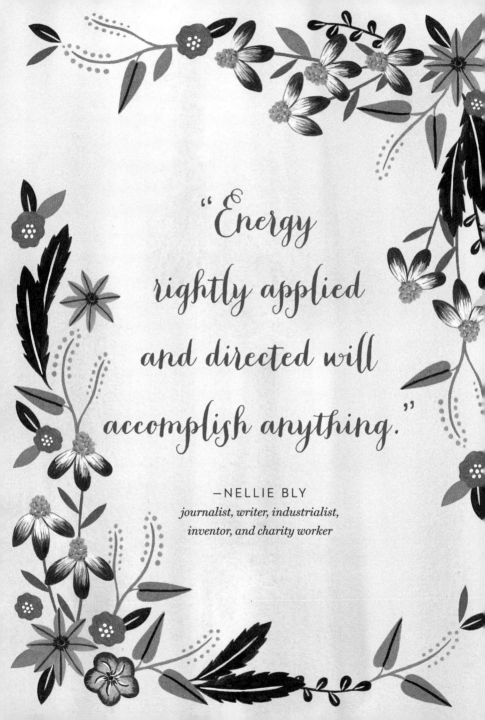

"Energy
rightly applied
and directed will
accomplish anything."

—NELLIE BLY
*journalist, writer, industrialist,
inventor, and charity worker*

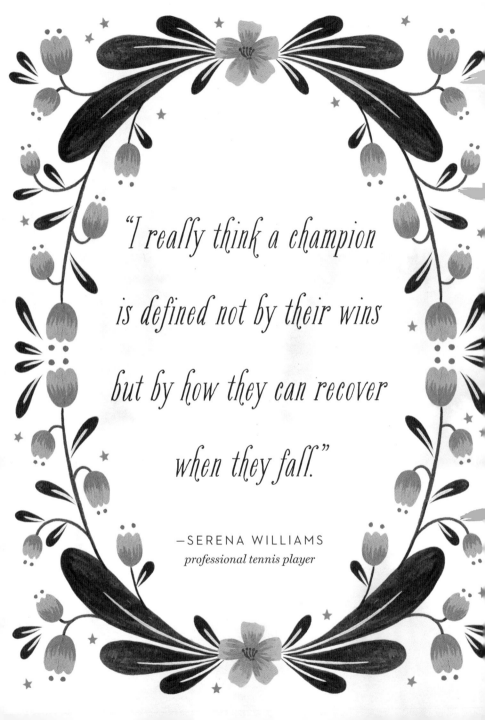

"I really think a champion is defined not by their wins but by how they can recover when they fall."

—SERENA WILLIAMS
professional tennis player

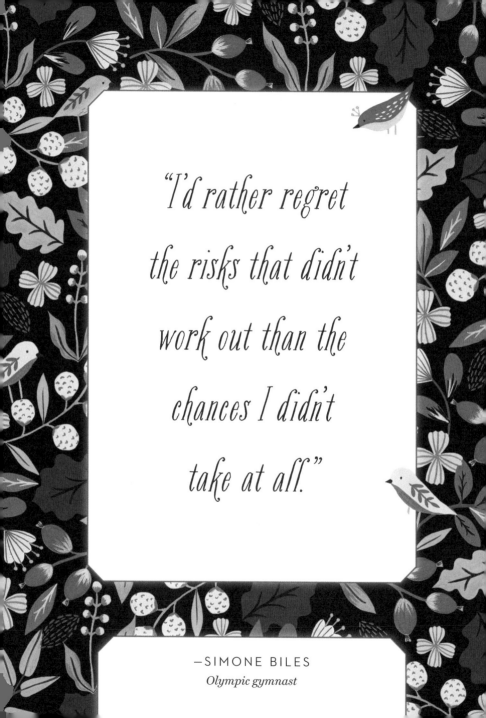

"I'd rather regret the risks that didn't work out than the chances I didn't take at all."

—SIMONE BILES

Olympic gymnast

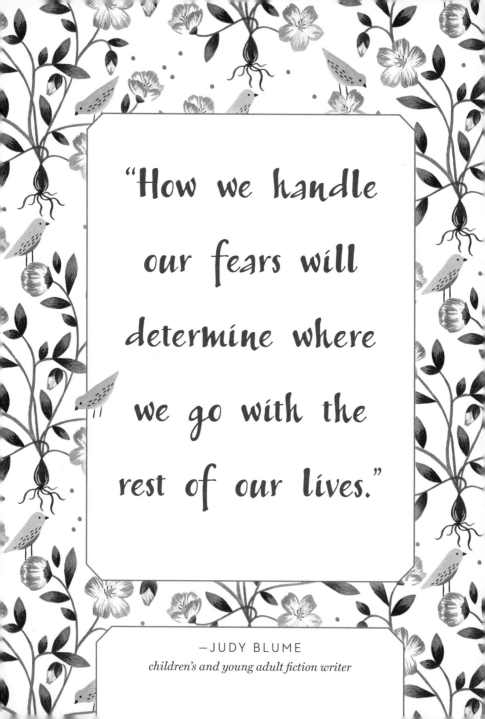

"How we handle our fears will determine where we go with the rest of our lives."

—JUDY BLUME

children's and young adult fiction writer

"Courage doesn't mean you don't get afraid. Courage means you don't let fear stop you."

—BETHANY HAMILTON
*professional surfer and
shark attack survivor*

"Humans are allergic to change. They love to say, 'We've always done it this way.' I try to fight that. That's why I have a clock on my wall that runs counter–clockwise."

–GRACE HOPPER
computer scientist and United States Navy
rear admiral

"Everyone shines, given the right lighting."

—SUSAN CAIN
writer and lecturer

"You don't make progress by standing on the sidelines, whimpering and complaining. You make progress by implementing ideas."

—SHIRLEY CHISHOLM
politician, activist, and author

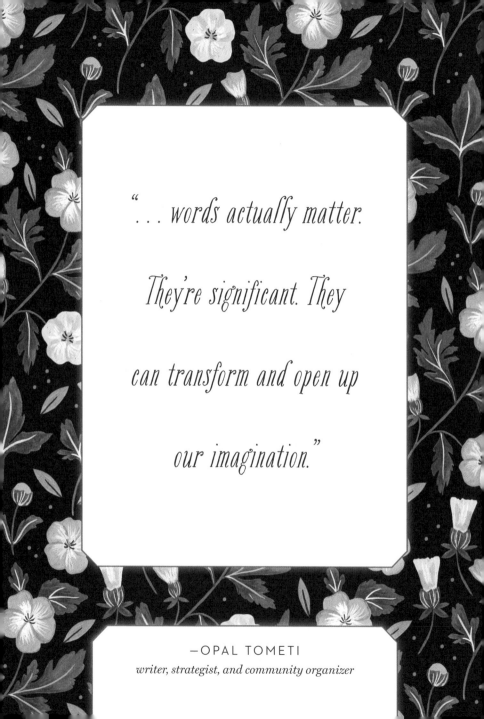

"... words actually matter.

They're significant. They

can transform and open up

our imagination."

—OPAL TOMETI
writer, strategist, and community organizer

"CONNECT DEEPLY WITH OTHERS. OUR HUMANITY IS THE ONE THING THAT WE ALL HAVE IN COMMON."

—MELINDA GATES
philanthropist

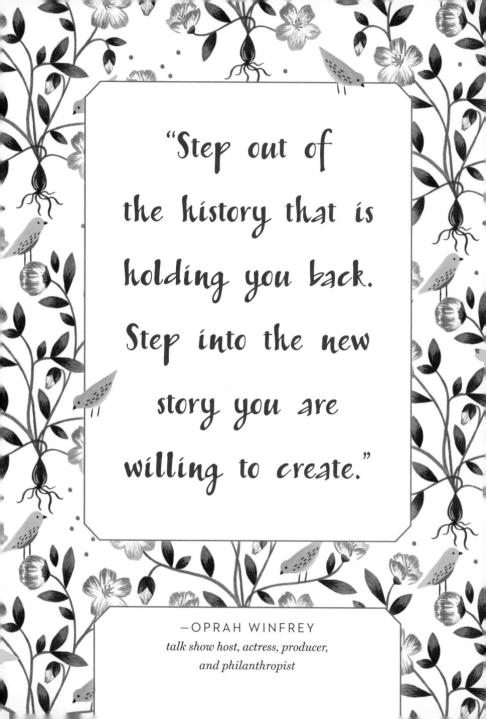

"Step out of
the history that is
holding you back.
Step into the new
story you are
willing to create."

—OPRAH WINFREY
*talk show host, actress, producer,
and philanthropist*

"Love is a fruit in season at all times and within reach of every hand. Anyone may gather it and no limit is set."

—MOTHER TERESA
Roman Catholic nun, missionary, and saint

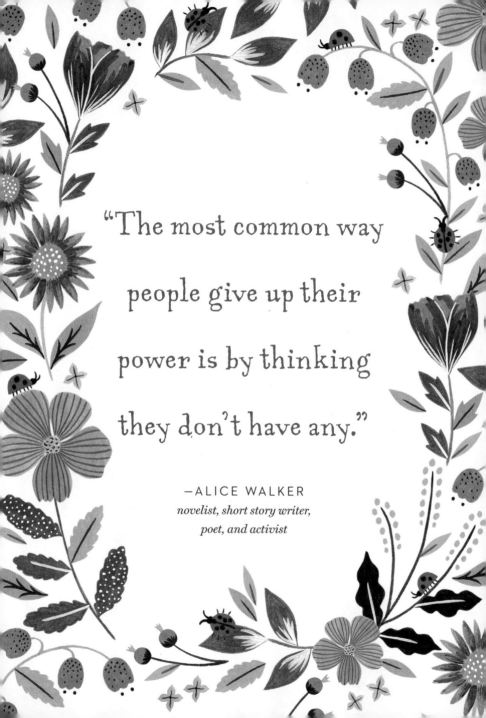

"The most common way people give up their power is by thinking they don't have any."

—ALICE WALKER
*novelist, short story writer,
poet, and activist*

"Lasting change
is a series
of compromises.
And compromise is all right,
as long your values
don't change."

—JANE GOODALL
*British primatologist, ethologist, anthropologist,
and UN Messenger of Peace*

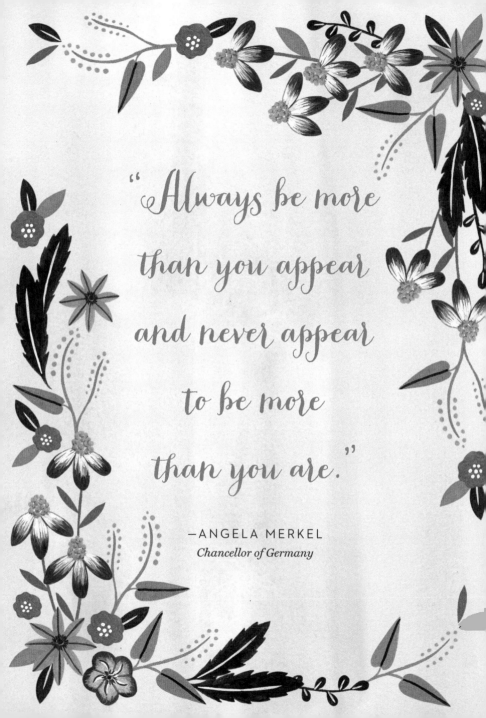

"Always be more than you appear and never appear to be more than you are."

—ANGELA MERKEL
Chancellor of Germany

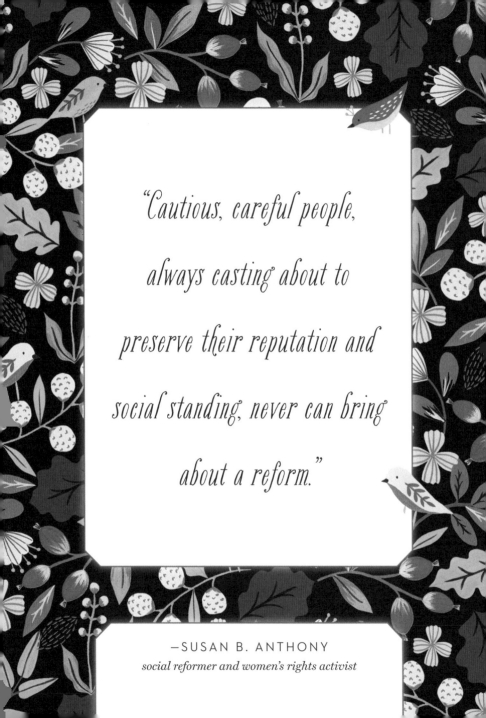

"Cautious, careful people, always casting about to preserve their reputation and social standing, never can bring about a reform."

—SUSAN B. ANTHONY
social reformer and women's rights activist

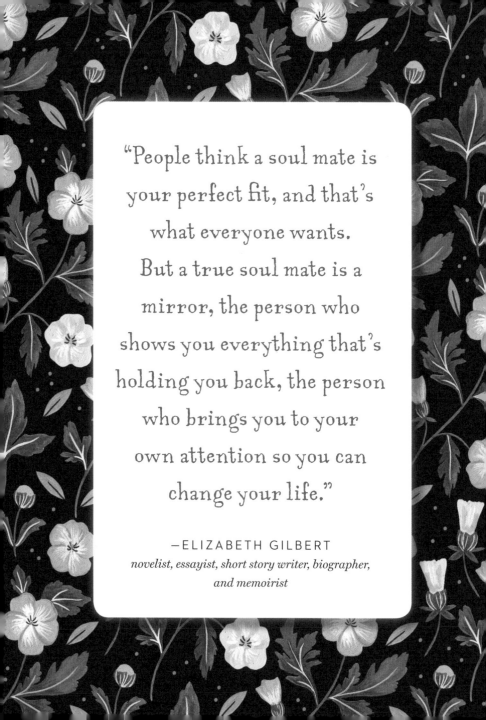

"People think a soul mate is your perfect fit, and that's what everyone wants. But a true soul mate is a mirror, the person who shows you everything that's holding you back, the person who brings you to your own attention so you can change your life."

—ELIZABETH GILBERT
novelist, essayist, short story writer, biographer, and memoirist